Collins

SNAP
REVISION
ALGEBRA

AQA GCSE Maths Foundation

AQA GCSE
MATHS
FOUNDATION

REVISE TRICKY
TOPICS IN A SNAP

Contents

Published by Collins
An imprint of HarperCollinsPublishers Ltd
1 London Bridge Street
London SE1 9GF

© HarperCollinsPublishers 2016

ISBN 9780008218041

First published 2016

10 9 8 7 6 5 4 3 2 1

British Library Cataloguing in Publication Data.

A CIP record of this book is available from the British Library.

Printed in Great Britain by Martins the Printers

ACKNOWLEDGEMENTS
The author and publisher are grateful to the copyright holders for permission to use quoted materials and images.

All images are © Shutterstock.com

Every effort has been made to trace copyright holders and obtain their permission for the use of copyright material. The author and publisher will gladly receive information enabling them to rectify any error or omission in subsequent editions. All facts are correct at time of going to press.

How To Use This Book

To get the most out of this revision guide, just work your way through the book in the order it is presented.

This is how it works:

Revise — Clear and concise revision notes help you get to grips with the topic

Revise — Key Points and Key Words explain the important information you need to know

Revise — A Quick Test at the end of every topic is a great way to check your understanding

Practise — Practice questions for each topic reinforce the revision content you have covered

Review — The Review section is a chance to revisit the topic to improve your recall in the exam

Basic Algebra

You must be able to:

- Use and understand algebraic notation and vocabulary
- Simplify and rearrange expressions
- Expand and factorise expressions
- Solve linear equations.

Basic Algebra

- 'Like terms' are terms with the same variable, e.g. $3x$ and $4x$ are like terms because they both contain the variable x.
- To simplify an expression you must collect like terms.
- When moving a term from one side of an equation to the other, you must carry out the inverse operation.

Key Point

When simplifying expressions, remember to:
- Use BIDMAS
- Show your working.

Simplify $3x + 3y - 7x + y$

$4y - 4x$

$3x - 7x = -4x$
$3y + y = 4y$

Simplify $9p^2 + 7p - qp + pq - p^2$

$8p^2 + 7p$

$qp = pq$

$9p^2 - p^2 = 8p^2$
$-qp + pq = 0$

- Substitution means replacing variables with numbers.

If $y = 4$ and $t = 6$, work out the value of $7y - 6t$

$7y - 6t = 7 \times 4 - 6 \times 6$
$= 28 - 36$
$= -8$

Key Point

An expression does not contain an = sign.

If $q = 5$, $r = 2$ and $z = -3$, work out the value of $rq + z^2$

$rq + z^2 = 2 \times 5 + (-3)^2$
$= 10 + 9$
$= 19$

Use brackets as the minus sign is also squared.

Key Point

Always apply the rules:
$- \times - = +$ $- \times + = -$
$+ \times + = +$ $+ \times - = -$

- To expand (multiply out) brackets, every term in the bracket is multiplied by the term outside the bracket.

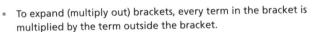

Expand $3(x + 2)$

$3x + 6$

Expand $5p(p - 2)$

$5p^2 - 10p$

$3 \times x = 3x$ and $3 \times 2 = +6$

$5p \times p = 5p^2$
$5p \times (-2) = -10p$

Expand and simplify $4y(2y - 3) - 3y(y - 2)$

$8y^2 - 12y - 3y^2 + 6y$
$= 5y^2 - 6y$

Note that $-3y \times -2 = +6y$

Factorisation

- Factorisation is the reverse of expanding brackets, i.e. you take out a common factor and put brackets into the expression.
- To factorise, you should look for common factors in every term.

Factorise $12x + 4$ ◄─── 4 is the HCF of 12 and 4.

$4(3x + 1)$

Factorise $3x^2 - 6x$

$3x(x - 2)$ ◄─── Remember $x^2 = x \times x$

Factorise $3p^3 - 2p^2 + 8p$

$p(3p^2 - 2p + 8)$

> **Key Point**
>
> To factorise completely, always take out the highest common factor, e.g. 3 is the HCF of 3 and 6.

Linear Equations

- A linear equation does not contain any variables with a power greater than 1.
- When you solve an equation, you are finding an unknown number, represented by a letter, e.g. x.

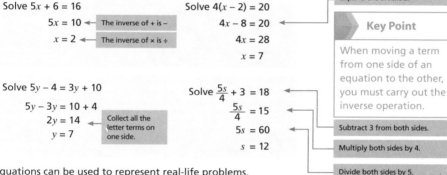

Solve $5x + 6 = 16$

$5x = 10$ ◄─ The inverse of + is −

$x = 2$ ◄─ The inverse of × is ÷

Solve $4(x - 2) = 20$ ◄─── Expand the brackets.

$4x - 8 = 20$

$4x = 28$

$x = 7$

> **Key Point**
>
> When moving a term from one side of an equation to the other, you must carry out the inverse operation.

Solve $5y - 4 = 3y + 10$

$5y - 3y = 10 + 4$

$2y = 14$ ◄─ Collect all the letter terms on one side.

$y = 7$

Solve $\frac{5s}{4} + 3 = 18$ ◄───

$\frac{5s}{4} = 15$ ◄───

$5s = 60$ ◄───

$s = 12$

Subtract 3 from both sides.

Multiply both sides by 4.

- Equations can be used to represent real-life problems.
- The equation should be rearranged to solve the problem.

Divide both sides by 5.

Mary bought nine candles. She used a £3 gift voucher as part payment. The balance left to pay was £5.55.

What was the cost of one candle (c)?

Use the information given to set up an equation.

$9c - 3 = 5.55$ ◄───

$9c = 8.55$ ◄───

$c = \frac{8.55}{9} = £0.95$ or 95p

Solve to find the cost of one candle.

> **Key Words**
>
> term
> variable
> expression
> equation
> inverse operation
> factorisation
> linear equation

Quick Test

1. Factorise $5x + 10$
2. Solve $7x - 2 = 12$
3. Simplify $2y - 7 + 4y + 2$
4. Work out the value of $3p^3 - 7q$, when $p = -4$ and $q = -3$.
5. Expand the following expression: $3t(4t - 1)$

Factorisation and Formulae

You must be able to:

- Expand the product of two binomials
- Factorise a quadratic expression
- Understand and use formulae
- Rearrange and change the subject of a formula.

Binomial Expansion

- A binomial is an expression that contains two terms, e.g. $x + 2$ or $3y - 4$.
- The product of two binomials is obtained when they are multiplied together, e.g. $(2r + 7)(3r - 6)$.
- To expand (or multiply out) the brackets, every term in the first set of brackets must be multiplied by every term in the second set of brackets.

Expand and simplify $(x + 2)(x + 6)$

×	x	$+2$
x	x^2	$+2x$
$+6$	$+6x$	$+12$

$x^2 + 2x + 6x + 12$
$= x^2 + 8x + 12$ ⟵ Simplify by collecting like terms.

Expand and simplify $(2y + 4)(3y - 2)$

×	$2y$	$+4$
$3y$	$6y^2$	$+12y$
-2	$-4y$	-8

$6y^2 + 12y - 4y - 8$
$= 6y^2 + 8y - 8$

> **Key Point**
>
> Take care over + and – signs.

Quadratic Factorisation

- An expression that contains a squared term is called quadratic.
- Some quadratic expressions can be written as a product of two binomials.
- When written in factorised form, the new expression is equivalent to the original quadratic.

> **Key Point**
>
> Check you have factorised correctly by expanding the brackets – your expressions should be equivalent.

Factorise $x^2 + 5x + 6$

$x^2 + 5x + 6$ ⟵ Find a pair of numbers with a sum of +5 and a product of +6.
$(x + 2)(x + 3)$ ⟵ $(+2) + (+3) = +5$ and $(+2) × (+3) = +6$

Factorise the expression $x^2 - 4x + 3$

×	x	-1
x	x^2	$-x$
-3	$-3x$	$+3$

$(x - 1)(x - 3)$

The missing terms need to have a product of $+3$ and a sum of -4, i.e. -1 and -3.

Write the expression as a product: the **first row** gives you the **first bracket** and the first column gives you the **second bracket**.

Changing the Subject of a Formula

- A formula is a way of describing a rule or fact.
- A formula is written as an algebraic equation.
- The subject of a formula appears once on the left-hand side.
- To change the subject, a formula must be rearranged using inverse operations.

Make p the subject of $5p - 7 = r$

$5p = r + 7$

$p = \dfrac{r + 7}{5}$

Key Point

When rearranging formulae remember to use inverse operations. Finish by writing the formula out with the new subject on the left-hand side.

This formula can be used to change temperature in degrees Fahrenheit to temperature in degrees Celsius:
$C = \frac{5}{9}(F - 32)$

In Iceland, the lowest recorded temperature on a certain day is $-20°C$.

What is this temperature in degrees Fahrenheit?

$-20 = \frac{5}{9}(F - 32)$

$-180 = 5(F - 32)$

$-36 = F - 32$

$F = -4°F$

The formula must be rearranged to find the value of F.

The answer is -4 degrees Fahrenheit.

Make r the subject of the formula $P = 3(r - 1)$

$\dfrac{P}{3} = r - 1$

$r = \dfrac{P}{3} + 1$

The formula for calculating the area of a circle is $A = \pi r^2$.

Make r the subject.

$\dfrac{A}{\pi} = r^2$

$r = \sqrt{\dfrac{A}{\pi}}$

π can be treated as a numerical term.

Only the positive root is needed as r is a length.

Key Words

binomial
expression
expand
quadratic
formula
subject
inverse operation

Quick Test

1. $T = 30w + 20$. Work out the value of w when $T = 290$.
2. Factorise $x^2 + 8x + 7$
3. Make q the subject of $6q - 5 = 2t$
4. Make y the subject of the formula $\dfrac{x + 2}{3} = 2(y - 1)$

Number Patterns and Sequences 1

Algebra

You must be able to:

- Work out missing terms in sequences using term-to-term rules and position-to-term rules
- Recognise and use arithmetic and geometric sequences
- Work out the rule for a given pattern.

Patterns in Number

- A sequence is a series of shapes or numbers that follow a particular pattern or rule.
- A term-to-term rule links the next term in the sequence to the previous one.
- A position-to-term rule, also called the *n*th term, can be used to work out any term in the sequence.

Write down the next two terms in the following sequence:

7, 11, 15, 19, __, __

The term-to-term rule is +4, so the next two terms are 23 and 27.

Write down the next two terms in the following sequence:

50, 25, 12.5, __, __

The term-to-term rule is ÷2, so the next two terms are 6.25 and 3.125.

General Rules from Given Patterns

Here is a sequence of patterns made from matchsticks:

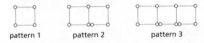

pattern 1   pattern 2   pattern 3

> **Key Point**
>
> When finding the term-to-term rule, remember to look at consecutive terms.

a) Draw the next pattern in the sequence.

b) Write down the sequence of numbers that represents the total number of matchsticks used in each pattern and state the term-to-term rule.

Pattern No.	1	2	3	4
No. of Matchsticks	4	7	10	13

The term-to-term rule is +3.

The nth term of a number sequence is $5n + 2$.

Write down the first five terms of the sequence.

$(5 \times 1) + 2 = 7$ ← To work out the first term, substitute $n = 1$ into the expression.

$(5 \times 2) + 2 = 12$ ←

7, 12, 17, 22, 27 ← To work out the second term, substitute $n = 2$ into the expression.

Continue until $n = 5$ to produce the first five terms of the sequence.

Number Sequences

- In an **arithmetic sequence**, there is a common difference between consecutive terms, e.g.

  5, 8, 11, 14, 17 … ← The terms have a common difference of +3.

- In a **geometric sequence**, each term is found by multiplying the previous term by a constant, e.g.

  20, 10, 5, 2.5, 1.25 … ← The constant (or ratio) is 0.5

The nth term of an arithmetic sequence is $4n - 1$.

a) Write down the term-to-term rule.

The sequence of numbers is 3, 7, 11, 15, 19 … ← Work out the first five terms.
The term-to-term rule is +4.

b) Marnie thinks that 50 is a number in this sequence.
Is Marnie correct? Give a reason for your answer.

$4n - 1 = 50$, $n = 12.75$ ← Use the nth term to find the value of n for an output of 50.
n is not a whole number, so 50 is **not** in this sequence.
Marnie is wrong.

Here is a geometric sequence: 4, 6, 9, __, 20.25

What is the missing term?

$\frac{6}{4} = \frac{9}{6} = 1.5$ ← Divide at least two given terms by the previous term to work out the ratio.

$9 \times 1.5 = 13.5$ ← Multiply by the ratio to find the missing term.

The missing term is 13.5

Quick Test

1. Here are the first five terms of a sequence: 16, 12, 8, 4, 0 …
   Write down the next two terms.
2. The nth term of a sequence is $5n - 7$.
   Work out the 1st term and the 10th term of this sequence.
3. In the sequence below the next pattern is formed by adding another layer of tiles around the previous pattern:

Work out how many tiles will be needed for the 6th pattern.

Key Words

sequence
term-to-term rule
position-to-term rule
nth term
arithmetic sequence
geometric sequence

Number Patterns and Sequences 2

You must be able to:

- Work out and use expressions to calculate the nth term of a linear sequence
- Recognise and use sequences of triangular numbers, squares, cubes and other special sequences.

Finding the nth Term of a Linear Sequence

- A number sequence that increases or decreases by the same amount each time is called a linear sequence.
- To work out the expression for the nth term in a linear sequence, look for a pattern in the numbers.
- Using a function machine to represent a sequence of numbers can help.

The first five terms of a sequence are: 9, 12, 15, 18, 21 …

What is the expression for the nth term of this sequence?

Input (n)	× 3 ($3n$)	Output
1	3	9
2	6	12
3	9	15
4	12	18
5	15	21
n	$3n$	$3n + 6$

The 'input' is the position of the term and the 'output' is the value of the term.

The difference between $3n$ and the output in each case is 6, so the expression for the nth term is **$3n + 6$**.

The term-to-term rule is +3, so the expression for the nth term starts with $3n$.

- The alternative method is to work out the zero term.

The first five terms of a sequence are: 20, 16, 12, 8, 4 …

What is the expression for the nth term of this sequence?

Input	Output
0	zero term
1	20
2	16
3	12
4	8
5	4
n	nth term

The zero term is $(20 + 4 =)$ 24

The difference between terms is –4.

The expression for the nth term is $-4n + 24$ or $24 - 4n$.

The nth term = 'the difference' × n + the zero term

> **Key Point**
>
> The zero term is the term that would come before the first term in a given sequence of numbers.

Special Sequences

- It is important to be able to recognise special sequences of numbers, e.g. the square numbers, the cube numbers, the triangular numbers and the Fibonacci sequence.

Here is a sequence of numbers: 1, 4, 9, 16, 25 …

Write down:

a) The next two terms.

36, 49 ←———————————————————— The sequence is the square numbers.

b) The nth term of the sequence.

The nth term is n^2.

Here is a sequence of numbers: 1, 8, 27, 64 …

Write down:

a) The next two terms.

125, 216 ←——————————————————— The sequence is the cube numbers.

b) The nth term of the sequence.

The nth term is n^3.

Here is a sequence of numbers: 1, 3, 6, 10, 15 …

Write down:

a) The next two terms.

21, 28 ←———————————————————— The sequence is the triangular numbers.

b) The nth term of the sequence.

The nth term is $\frac{n}{2}(n + 1)$.

Write down the next two terms in the following sequence:
1, 1, 2, 3, 5, 8, 13, 21 …

34, 55 ←———————————————————— This is the Fibonacci sequence. The next term is found by adding the previous two terms together.

Quick Test

1. Write down the next two terms in the following sequence:
   6, 9, 12, 15, __, __
2. a) Write down the nth term for the following sequence:
      7, 10, 13, 16, 19 …
   b) Work out the 50th term in this sequence.
3. Write down the nth term for the following sequence:
   0, 3, 8, 15, 24 …

Key Words

linear sequence
zero term
Fibonacci sequence

Practice Questions

Basic Algebra & Factorisation and Formulae

1 Expand $5(x + 6)$ 📱 [2]

2 Factorise $15x + 10$ 📱 [1]

3 Expand $6(5 - 2x)$ 📱 [2]

4 Make t the subject of $p = 4t - q$ 📱 [2]

5 Simplify $5x - 2y + 4x + 6y$ 📱 [2]

6 Simplify $5 - 3z + y - 5z + 7 + 3y$ 📱 [2]

7 Simplify $3x^2 + 3x + x^2 + 4 - x$
Circle your answer. 📱

$10x + 4$ $4x^2 + 2x + 4$ $6x^2 + 4$ $10x^2$ [1]

8 Work out the value of $3z^2 - 2q + 5$, when $z = -2$ and $q = -3$.
Circle your answer. 📱

11   23   35   47 [1]

9 Solve $4(2b - 3) = 2$ 📱 [2]

10 Solve $3(p + 2) = 2(p + 3)$ 📱 [2]

11 Solve $\frac{5}{2}x - \frac{1}{3} = \frac{2}{3}x + \frac{1}{2}$ 📱 [3]

12 Expand $6(x - 5y + 6)$ 📱 [2]

13 Expand $6p - 4(q - 3)$ 📱 [2]

14 Factorise completely $4xyz - 4xz$ 📱 [2]

15 Factorise $x^2 + 3x + 2$ 📱 [2]

16 Write $3(2x - 5) + 4(x + 3) - 4x$ in the form $a(bx + c)$, where a, b and c are integers. 📱 [3]

17 Look at the options below and circle the formula. 📱

$x^4 - x^2$ $2x - x = x$ $3x - 5 = 10$ $A = \frac{1}{2}(a + b)h$ [1]

Total Marks _____ / 32

Number Patterns and Sequences 1 & 2

1 For each of the following sequences write down **i)** the next two terms in the sequence and **ii)** the term-to-term rule:

    a) 5, 8, 11, 14, 17, __ , __   [2]

    b) 16, 12, 8, 4, 0, __ , __   [2]

    c) 189, 63, 21, 7, $\frac{7}{3}$, __ , __   [2]

2 Here is a sequence:

    20, 16, 12, 8, 4 ...

    Circle the expression for the nth term of the sequence.

    $20n - 4$ $4n + 20$ $4n - 24$ $24 - 4n$ [1]

3 Work out the first five terms in the sequence with the nth term $3n - 5$.   [2]

4 The first five terms of an arithmetic sequence are 14, 17, 20, 23, 26 ...

    a) Write an expression for the nth term of this sequence.   [2]

    b) Calculate the 100th term in this sequence.   [1]

5 **a)** A sequence of numbers is given as 5, 8, 12, 17 ...

    Write down the next two terms in the sequence.   [2]

    b) A second sequence of numbers is given as 2, 3, 2, 3, 2, 3 ...

    Write down the 100th term.   [1]

6 Here is a sequence of patterns made using matchsticks.

    a) Draw the next two patterns in the sequence.   [2]

    b) Write down the rule for the number of matchsticks required for pattern number n.   [2]

    c) Use the rule to work out how many matchsticks are required for pattern 100.   [1]

Total Marks _____ / 20

Linear Graphs

You must be able to:

- Work with coordinates in all four quadrants
- Plot graphs of linear functions
- Work out the equation of a line through two given points or through one point with a given gradient
- Work out the gradient and y-intercept of a straight line in the form $y = mx + c$.

Drawing Linear Graphs from Points

- **Linear graphs** are straight-line graphs.
- The equation of a straight-line graph is usually given in the form $y = mx + c$, where m is the **gradient** of the line and c is the **intercept** of the y-axis.
- $y = mx + c$ is a function of x, where the **input** is the x-coordinate and the **output** is the y-coordinate.

Write down the gradient and y-intercept of the line of equation $y = 5x + 1$.

The gradient is 5.
The y-intercept is $(0,1)$.

Draw the graph of the equation $y = 2x + 5$.
Use values of x from –3 to 3.

x $\boxed{-3}$ $\xrightarrow{\times 2}$ $\boxed{-6}$ $\xrightarrow{+5}$ $\boxed{-1}$ y

x	–3	0	3
y	–1	5	11

> **Key Point**
>
> To draw a straight line, only two coordinates are needed.

You can set up a flow chart to work out the y-coordinates.

Draw a table of values. Include a third value as a check.

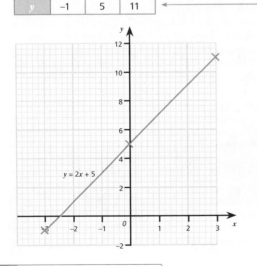

$y = 2x + 5$

The Cover-Up Method

- Another method that can be used to draw a graph is the cover-up method.
- This can be used for equations in the form $ax + by = c$.

Draw the graph of the equation $2x + 3y = 6$.

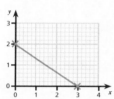

$3y = 6$ ← | Cover up the x term and solve to find y.
$y = 2$ The y-intercept is (0, 2).

$2x = 6$ ← | Cover up the y term and solve to find x.
$x = 3$ The x-intercept is (3, 0).

Finding the Equation of a Line

- To find the equation of a straight line in the form $y = mx + c$, work out the gradient and y-intercept.

Work out the equation of the line that joins the points (1, 20) and (4, 5).

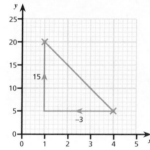

Gradient $= \dfrac{15}{-3}$

$= -5$

$y = mx + c$

$y = -5x + c$ ← | To work out the value of c, substitute in the gradient and point (1, 20) or (4, 5).

$20 = -5 \times 1 + c$

$c = 25$

The equation of the line is $y = -5x + 25$ ← | Substitute your values for m and c into the equation.

Key Point

Gradient $= \dfrac{\text{Change in } y}{\text{Change in } x}$

If the line slopes down from left to right, the gradient is negative.

See p.18–19 for more information on gradients.

Quick Test

1. Draw the graph with equation $y = 4x + 1$ from $x = 0$ to $x = 6$.
2. Write down the gradient and y-intercept of the line with equation $y = 5 - 2x$.
3. Work out the equation of the line that joins the points (5, 7) and (3, 10).

Key Words

linear graph
gradient
intercept
input
output

Graphs of Quadratic Functions

You must be able to:

- Recognise, sketch and interpret graphs of quadratic functions
- Identify and interpret roots, intercepts and turning points of quadratic functions
- Work out roots using algebraic methods
- Work out turning points.

Plotting Quadratic Graphs

- A quadratic equation is an equation that contains an unknown term with a power of 2, e.g. x^2.
- You can use a table of values to draw quadratic graphs.

Draw the graph of the function $y = 2x^2 + 1$.

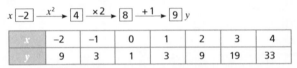

$x \boxed{-2} \xrightarrow{x^2} \boxed{4} \xrightarrow{\times 2} \boxed{8} \xrightarrow{+1} \boxed{9} \, y$

x	−2	−1	0	1	2	3	4
y	9	3	1	3	9	19	33

> **Key Point**
>
> Remember to use BIDMAS when working out the y-coordinates.

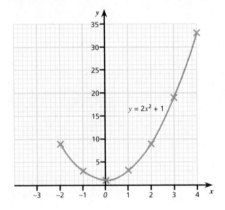

$y = 2x^2 + 1$

The Significant Points of a Quadratic Curve

- A sketch is used to show the shape and significant points on a graph, but it is not an accurate drawing.
- To sketch a quadratic, work out the roots, the intercept and the turning point, i.e. maximum or minimum point.
- The roots are found by solving the quadratic when $y = 0$.
- Because quadratic curves are symmetrical, the turning point is halfway between the two roots.

> **Key Point**
>
> All quadratic graphs have a line of symmetry, which passes through the turning point.
>
> The roots of a quadratic equation are the points where the graph crosses the x-axis. Not all quadratic curves will have roots.

Sketch the graph of equation $y = x^2 + 5x + 4$.

Roots:

$x^2 + 5x + 4 = 0$ ← Work out the values for x when $y = 0$.

$(x + 4)(x + 1) = 0$

$x = -4$ and $x = -1$

y-intercept:

$y = 4$

y-intercept is $(0, 4)$. ← Substitute $x = 0$ into the equation.

Turning Point:

$x = -4$ and $x = -1$, therefore $x = -2.5$ ← The value of x for the turning point is in the middle of the two roots.

$y = (-2.5)^2 + (5 \times -2.5) + 4$

$\quad = -2.25$

Turning point is $(-2.5, -2.25)$. Substitute the value of x into the equation.

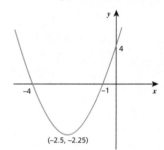

> **Key Point**

If the value of the x^2 term is **positive**, the graph will have a **minimum** point. If the value of the x^2 term is **negative**, the graph will have a **maximum** point.

> **Quick Test**

1. Sketch the graph of the equation $y = x^2 - 3x + 2$.
2. Draw the graph with the equation $y = x^2 - 6$.
3. Draw the graph of $y = 3x^2 - 2x + 1$, for values of x between -2 and 2.
4. Write down the coordinates of the roots and turning point of the quadratic curve shown.

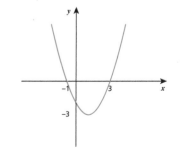

> **Key Words**

quadratic equation
quadratic graph
roots
intercept
turning point
maximum point
minimum point

Uses of Graphs

You must be able to:

- Use the form $y = mx + c$ to identify parallel lines
- Interpret the gradient of a straight-line graph as a rate of change
- Recognise and interpret graphs that illustrate direct and inverse proportion.

Parallel Lines

- **Parallel** lines travel in the same direction and have the same gradient.

Write down the gradient of the line that is parallel to the line with the equation $y = 6x + 2$.

The line has a gradient of +6, so the line that is parallel to it also has a gradient of +6.

> **Key Point**
>
> The gradient of a straight line in the form $y = mx + c$ is m.

Write down the gradient of the line that is parallel to the line with the equation $y = 7 - 2x$.

The line has a gradient of –2, so the line that is parallel to it also has a gradient of –2.

Work out the equation of the line that goes through the point (2, 9) and is parallel to the line with equation $y = 7x + 10$.

$y = mx + c$
$y = 7x + c$ ← — — — — — — — — — — Substitute in $m = 7$.
$9 = (7 \times 2) + c$ ← — — — — — — — — Goes through the point (2, 9), so $x = 2$ when $y = 9$.
$c = -5$
The equation of the parallel line is $y = 7x - 5$.

Gradient of a Line

- The **rate of change** is the rate at which one quantity changes in relation to another.
- The gradient of a straight-line graph represents a rate of change – it describes how the variable on the y-axis changes when the variable on the x-axis is increased by 1.

$$\text{Gradient} = \frac{\text{Change in } y}{\text{Change in } x}$$

Write down the gradient of the line that joins points (1, 3) and (5, 9).

Gradient = $\frac{6}{4}$

= 1.5

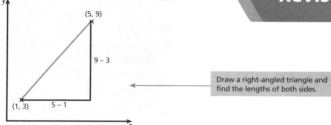

Draw a right-angled triangle and find the lengths of both sides.

The graph shows the volume of liquid in a container over time.

What is the rate of change?

Gradient = $\frac{4}{5}$

= 0.8cm³/s

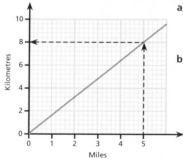

The gradient is the rate of change.

Real-Life Uses of Graphs

The graph below is the conversion graph between miles and kilometres.

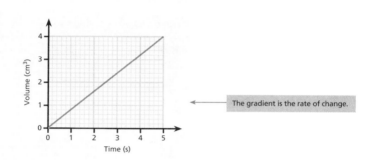

a) How many kilometres are there in 5 miles?

5 miles = 8km

Read from graph.

b) What is the gradient of the line?

Gradient = $\frac{8}{5}$

= 1.6

1 mile = 1.6km

Quick Test

1. Work out the equation of the line that is parallel to the line $y = -2x + 6$ and goes through the point (4, 7).
2. Write down the gradient of the line that joins points (4, 7) and (6, 11).

Key Words

parallel
rate of change

Other Graphs

You must be able to:

- Recognise, draw and interpret cubic and reciprocal graphs
- Interpret distance–time graphs and velocity–time graphs
- Work out acceleration from a velocity–time graph
- Work out speed from a distance–time graph.

Distance–Time Graphs

- A distance–time graph shows distance travelled in relation to a fixed point (starting point) over a period of time.
- The gradient of a straight line joining two points is the speed of travel between those two points.

> **Key Point**
>
> $\text{Speed} = \dfrac{\text{Distance}}{\text{Time}}$

The graph below shows Val's car journey from St Bees to Cockermouth and back.

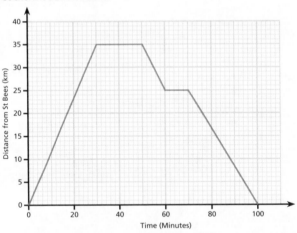

a) Val sets off at 12 noon and travels directly to Cockermouth. At what time does she arrive?

Val travels for 30 minutes so arrives at 12.30pm.

b) For how long does Val stop in Cockermouth?

20 minutes ◄

> This is represented by the horizontal line on the graph – where the distance does not change.

c) Val begins her journey home but stops to fill up with petrol.

Calculate the average speed of Val's journey from the petrol station to home in kilometres per hour.

$\text{Speed} = \dfrac{\text{Distance}}{\text{Time}} = \dfrac{25}{0.5}$ ◄

> Convert minutes into hours.

$= 50\text{km/h}$

Velocity–Time Graphs

- **Velocity** has both magnitude (size) and direction.
- The magnitude of velocity is called speed.
- The gradient of a straight line joining two points is the acceleration between those two points.
- Area Under Graph = Distance Travelled.

The graph below shows part of the journey of a car.

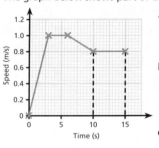

a) For how many seconds does the car decelerate?

4 seconds

b) What is the distance travelled in the last five seconds of the journey?

5 × 0.8 = 4m

c) What is the acceleration of the car in the first three seconds of the journey?

The acceleration is $\frac{1}{3}$ m/s²

Between 6 seconds and 10 seconds, there is a negative gradient so the car is decelerating.

This is the area of the rectangle under that part of the line.

This is the gradient of the line.

Other Graphs

- A **cubic function** is one that contains an x^3 term.
- A **reciprocal** function takes the form $y = \frac{a}{x}$.

Cubic Function

Reciprocal Function

Quick Test

1. Plot the graph $y = 3x^3 - 5$ for values −2 to 2.
2. Below is a graph for the journey of a car.

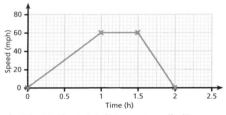

a) What is the total distance travelled?
b) For how many minutes is the car decelerating?

Review Questions

Basic Algebra & Factorisation and Formulae

1 There are k children in a room.
The number of children who wear glasses is g.

Write an expression in terms of k and g for the number of children who **do not** wear glasses. [1]

2 Simplify $7x - 2y + 5x - 3y$ [2]

3 Work out the value of the following expression when $a = -3$.
$$\frac{4a^2 - a^3}{a^4}$$
Circle your answer.

$\frac{1}{9}$ $\quad\quad\quad -\frac{1}{9}$ $\quad\quad\quad \frac{7}{9}$ $\quad\quad\quad -\frac{7}{9}$ [1]

4 Solve $2x + 6 = 5x - 10$ [3]

5 Factorise $5ab - 3b^2c$ [1]

6 Solve $4(x - 3) = 10$ [3]

7 Solve $\frac{x}{3} + 3 = 1$ and circle your answer.

$x = 0$ $\quad\quad\quad x = 12$ $\quad\quad\quad x = -6$ $\quad\quad\quad x = 8$ [1]

8 The shape below is a rectangle.

$6x + 5$

$3x + 2$

Mitan thinks the correct expression for the perimeter of the rectangle is $9x + 7$.

a) Mitan is wrong. Write down the correct expression for the perimeter. [1]

b) The perimeter of the rectangle is 56cm. Work out the value of x. [2]

9 The formula for the volume of a cylinder is $V = \pi r^2 h$.

a) Make r the subject of the formula. [2]

b) Work out the value of r when $V = 50$ and $h = 10$. [2]

Total Marks _____ / 19

Number Patterns and Sequences 1 & 2

1 The first term that the following two sequences have in common is 17.

8, 11, 14, 17, 20 …

1, 5, 9, 13, 17 …

Work out the next term that the two sequences have in common.
You must show your working. [2]

2 Regular pentagons of side length 1cm are joined together to make a pattern.

a) Use the patterns to complete the table below.

Pattern Number	Perimeter (cm)
1	
2	
3	
4	
60	
n	

[2]

b) What is the maximum number of pentagons that could be used to give a perimeter less than 1500cm? [2]

3 Write down the first three terms in the sequence with the nth term $n^2 - 6$. [2]

4 Write down the next two terms in the sequence below:

4, 6, 10, 18, 34 … [2]

Total Marks _____ / 10

Linear Graphs & Graphs of Quadratic Functions

1 A straight-line graph has the equation $y = 3x + 7$.

    a) To plot the graph, you need to work out values of x and y for the equation.

       Draw a flow diagram that can be used to work out values for x and y, where x is the input and y is the output. [2]

    b) Use your flow diagram to complete the table below. [2]

x	−3	−2	−1	0	1	2	3
$y = 3x + 7$	−2				10		

    c) Draw the graph of $y = 3x + 7$ for values of x from −3 to 3. [2]

2 **a)** Sketch the graph of $y = x^2 + 3x + 2$.
       Clearly label the points where the graph crosses the axes. [3]

    b) Write down the x-coordinate of the turning point of the graph. [1]

3 Draw the graph of $y = 4x - 2$ for values of x from −4 to 4. [2]

4 Draw the graph of the function with gradient 5 and y-intercept (0, 3) for values of x between −2 and 2. [2]

5 Write down the gradient and y-intercept of the graph with equation $y = 5 - 2x$. [1]

6 Draw the graph with equation $y = 3x^2 - 2x + 1$ for values of x from −3 to 3. [2]

7 Work out the equation of the line that joins the points (−3, 5) and (3, −1). [3]

8 Work out the equation of the line shown. [3]

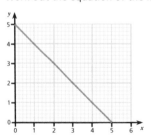

Total Marks _____ / 23

Uses of Graphs & Other Graphs

1 A line is parallel to the line of equation $y = 3x - 2$ and goes through the point (1, 5).

Work out the equation of the line. [3]

2 Gemma, Naval and Esmai entered a five-mile cycling race. The graph below shows the race.

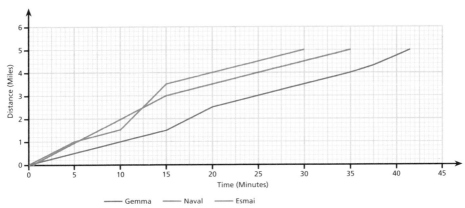

—— Gemma —— Naval —— Esmai

a) Who won the race? [1]

b) What speed was Naval travelling at for the last 20 minutes before he finished?
Give your answer in miles per hour. [2]

c) Between what times was Gemma travelling her fastest?
Give a reason for your answer. [2]

d) How many minutes after the race started did the winner move into the lead? [1]

e) Describe the race. [3]

3 The graph below shows the journey of a train. Work out the total distance travelled. [3]

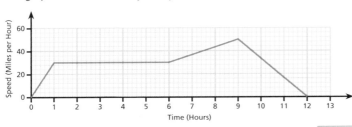

Total Marks _____ / 15

Inequalities

You must be able to:

- Solve linear inequalities in one or two variables
- Represent solutions to inequalities on number lines or graphs.

Linear Inequalities

- The solution to an inequality can be shown on a number line.

 means $x <$ means $x >$

means $x \leqslant$ means $x \geqslant$

> **Key Point**
>
> $>$ means greater than
> $\geqslant$ means greater than or equal to
> $<$ means less than
> $\leqslant$ means less than or equal to

Solve these inequalities and show the solutions on a number line:

a) $x + 3 > 4$

$x > 4 - 3$

$x > 1$

b) $2(x + 4) \leqslant 18$

$x + 4 \leqslant 9$

$x \leqslant 5$

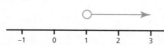

Work out all the possible integer values of n for these inequalities:

a) $-4 < n < 4$

$n = -3, -2, -1, 0, 1, 2, 3$

b) $-3 < 10n \leqslant 53$

$-0.3 < n \leqslant 5.3$ ◄ Divide each part of the inequality by 10.

$n = 0, 1, 2, 3, 4, 5$ ◄ n must be a whole number.

Graphical Inequalities

- The graph of the equation $y = 6$ is a line.
- The graph of the inequality $y > 6$ is a region, which has the line $y = 6$ as a boundary.
- For inequalities $>$ and $<$ the boundary line is **not included** in the solution and is shown as a **dashed line**.
- For inequalities $\geqslant$ and $\leqslant$ the boundary line is **included** in the solution and is shown as a **solid line**.

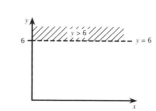

On a graph, show the region that satisfies $x \geq 0$, $x + y < 3$ and $y > 3x - 1$.

$x + y = 3$

$\quad y = 3 - x$

x	0	1	2
y	3	2	1

$y = 3x - 1$

x	0	1	2
y	−1	2	5

> Work out values of y for $x + y = 3$ and $y = 3x - 1$. You need three values.

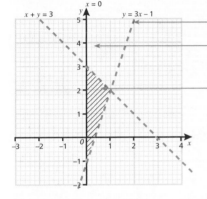

> Draw the dashed lines $x + y = 3$ and $y = 3x - 1$.

> The line $x = 0$ is the y-axis.

> This is the region that satisfies all three inequalities.

- The region that satisfies $x \geq 0$ is to the right of the y-axis. All the points in this region have a value of x greater than 0.
- The region that satisfies $x + y < 3$ is below the line $x + y = 3$. When the values of x and y are added together, the result is always less than 3.
- The region that satisfies $y > 3x - 1$ is above the line $y = 3x - 1$.
- The overlap of the three regions is the region that satisfies all three inequalities.

Quick Test

1. Solve the inequality $2x - 5 < 9$ and show the solution on a number line.
2. Write down all the possible integer values for $-5 \leq y < -1$.
3. Which inequality sign is missing between the numbers?
   a) $-3.2 \_\_ -3.3$
   b) $3.2 \_\_ 3.3$

Key Words

inequality
region

Quadratic and Simultaneous Equations

You must be able to:

- Solve quadratic equations by factorising
- Solve two simultaneous equations
- Find approximate solutions to quadratic and simultaneous equations by using a graph.

Factorisation

- When solving a quadratic equation by factorisation (see p.5–7), make sure it equals zero first.

Solve the equation $x^2 + 4x + 3 = 0$ by factorisation.

×	x	+1
x	x^2	$+x$
+3	$+3x$	+3

$(x + 1)(x + 3) = 0$
$x + 1 = 0 \qquad x + 3 = 0$
$x = -1 \qquad x = -3$

Set up and complete a table. The missing terms need to have a product of +3 and a sum of +4.

First row = first bracket; first column = second bracket.

The Method of Intersection

- Plotting a graph of a quadratic equation can give zero, one or two solutions for x when $y = 0$.
- The solutions are given by the curve's points of intersection with the x-axis.

Find approximate solutions to the equation $x^2 - 5x + 1 = 0$ by plotting a graph.

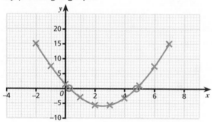

There are two solutions: $x = 0.2$ or $x = 4.8$

These solutions are approximate.

> **Key Point**
>
> If two brackets have a product of zero, one of the brackets must equal 0.

> **Key Point**
>
> The points of intersection with the x-axis are called roots.

Simultaneous Equations

- Simultaneous equations can be solved by elimination.

Solve the following simultaneous equations:

$3x - y = 18$ Equation 1
$x + y = 10$ Equation 2
$4x = 28$ $7 + y = 10$
$x = 7$ $y = 3$

> **Key Point**
>
> Solutions to simultaneous equations always come in pairs.

Add equation 1 and equation 2 to eliminate the y terms.

Substitute your value for x into one of the equations.

Annabel buys three pears and two apples for £1.20.
David buys four pears and three apples for £1.65.

Work out the cost of one apple and one pear.

$$3p + 2a = 120 \quad \text{Equation 1}$$
$$4p + 3a = 165 \quad \text{Equation 2}$$
Equation 1 × 4: $12p + 8a = 480$
Equation 2 × 3: $12p + 9a = 495$
$$a = 15$$
$$3p + (2 \times 15) = 120$$
$$p = 30$$

An apple costs 15p and a pear costs 30p.

> Form two equations with the information given.

> Multiply so that the p terms match. Remember to multiply all terms.

> Subtract equation 1 from equation 2.

> Substitute your value for a into one of the equations and solve.

Solve the following equations simultaneously:

$$y = 2x + 1 \quad \text{Equation 1}$$
$$3y + x = 10 \quad \text{Equation 2}$$

$$3(2x + 1) + x = 10$$
$$6x + 3 + x = 10$$
$$7x + 3 = 10$$
$$7x = 7$$
$$x = 1$$
$$y = (2 \times 1) + 1$$
$$y = 3$$

> Substitute $y = 2x + 1$ into equation 2.

> Substitute your value for x into equation 1 to find y.

Solve the simultaneous equations:
$$y = 3x^2$$
$$y + 5x = 3$$

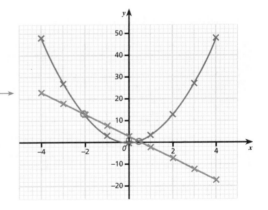

> You can plot graphs and find the points of intersection. However the solutions are only approximate.

The points of intersection are
(−2.1, 13.5) and (0.5, 1).

So, the two approximate solutions are
$x = -2.1$ and $y = 13.5$ or $x = 0.5$ and $y = 1$.

Quick Test

1. Solve the equation $x^2 = 2x + 5$ by the method of intersection.
2. Solve the simultaneous equations:
   $2x + y = 5$
   $x + y = 3$

Key Words

factorisation
intersection
simultaneous equation

Review Questions

Linear Graphs & Graphs of Quadratic Functions

1 Work out the equation of the line that joins the points $\left(\frac{2}{3}, 8\right)$ and $\left(\frac{5}{6}, 5\right)$. [3]

2 Work out the equation of the line drawn below. [3]

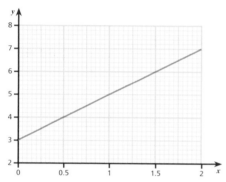

3 Sketch the graph of the function $y = x^2 + 4x + 3$, clearly stating the roots and the coordinates of the turning point. [3]

4 The equation of a line is $4y = 3x + 1$.

Work out the gradient and y-intercept of the line. [2]

5 A curve has the equation $y = x^2 + ax + b$.
The curve crosses the x-axis at the points $(-7, 0)$ and $(1, 0)$.

a) Work out the values of a and b. [3]

b) Work out the x-coordinate of the turning point. [1]

6 **a)** Sketch the graph $y = \frac{1}{x}$. [1]

b) On the same axes sketch the graph $y = -\frac{1}{x}$. [1]

7 Sketch the graph of $y = x^3$. [1]

Total Marks _____ / 18

Uses of Graphs & Other Graphs

1 The graph below shows the journey of a car.

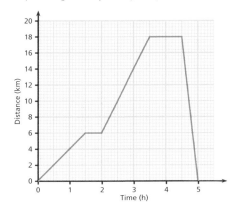

a) What is the greatest speed at which the car travels during the journey? [1]

b) Why does the graph have a gradient of zero between 2.5 and 3 hours? [1]

c) Calculate the total distance travelled by the car. [3]

2 The graph shows Sophie's journey to her friend's house. Her friend lives 18km away.
Sophie began her journey at 1pm.

a) Sophie stopped on the way to see her friend.

  i) How is this shown on the graph? [1]

  ii) How long did Sophie stop for? [1]

b) At what time did Sophie arrive at her
   friend's house? [1]

c) Sophie was picked up from her friend's house
   by her mum.

  i) Calculate the average speed, in km/h, of
     her journey home. [2]

  ii) At what time did Sophie arrive home? [1]

3 Work out the equation of the line that is parallel to the line $y = 2x - 5$ and goes through the
point (3, 6). [3]

> Total Marks _____ / 14

Practice Questions

Inequalities

1 Write down all the integer values for m that satisfy $-1 \leqslant m < 4$. [1]

2 Solve $2x - 6 > 2$ [2]

3 Write down all the possible integer values for y if $12 \leqslant 3y \leqslant 36$. [2]

4

Write down the inequality represented by the number line. [2]

5 If $-6 \leqslant d \leqslant 2$ and $-5 \leqslant e \leqslant 5$, work out: 🔢

a) The largest possible value of $d \times e$. [1]

b) The smallest possible value of $d \times e$. [1]

6 a) Solve the Inequality $7x + 6 \geqslant 41$ 🔢 [1]

b) Write down all the integer values of x if $-2 < x \leqslant 2$. 🔢 [1]

7 State whether each of the following statements is true or false: 🔢

a) $4 > 4.01$ [1]

b) $2.1 < 2.09$ [1]

c) When $-1 < y < 4$, y has the values of 0, 1, 2, 3 [1]

Total Marks .... /14

Quadratic and Simultaneous Equations

1 Solve the equation $3x^2 = 27$
Circle your answer.

$x = 3$ $\qquad$ $x = -3$ $\qquad$ $x = \dfrac{\pm\sqrt{27}}{3}$ $\qquad$ $x = \pm 3$ $\qquad$ [1]

2 **a)** On the same set of axes, draw the graphs $y = 2x^2$ and $y = 3x + 2$ [2]

   b) Use your graph to solve the equation $2x^2 = 3x + 2$ [2]

3 Solve the simultaneous equations: [4]

   $2x + y = 1$

   $y = x - 2$

4 **a)** Factorise $x^2 + 2x - 8$ [1]

   b) Use your answer to part **a)** to help solve the equation $x^2 + 2x - 8 = 0$ [2]

5 Rebecca goes to the greengrocer's shop and buys three apples and two pears. She pays £2.20.

   Mandeep goes to the same greengrocer's shop and buys six apples and two pears.
   She pays £3.40.

   Work out the cost of one pear and the cost of one apple.
   You **must** show all your working. [4]

6 Solve the simultaneous equations:

   $x + y = 5$

   $2x - y = 7$ [4]

7 Solve the simultaneous equations:

   $4y + 3x = 17$

   $3y + 2x = 12$ [4]

8 The graph has the equation $y = x^2 + 2x - 2$

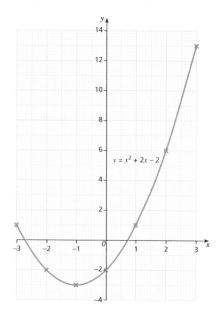

a) Using the graph, estimate solutions to the equation $x^2 + 2x - 2 = 0$ [2]

b) On the same axes, draw the graph of equation $y = x - 1$ [1]

c) Use your graphs to solve the equation $x^2 + 2x - 2 = x - 1$ [2]

9 Solve the simultaneous equations:

$4x + y = 17$

$2x + y = 9$ [4]

10 Solve the following equation by factorising:

$x^2 + 3x = 4$ [3]

11 Circle the correct value of a for:

$x^2 + 7x + 6 = (x + a)(x + 1)$

$a = 6$ $a = 8$ $a = 7$ $a = 3$ [1]

Total Marks _____ / 37

Inequalities

1. Write down all the possible integer values of n if $3 \leqslant n \leqslant 7$. [1]

2. Solve $3x + 4 > 25$ [2]

3. Work out all the possible integer values of y if $15 \leqslant 5y \leqslant 35$. [2]

4. A TV salesperson is set a target to sell more than six televisions a week.
   The manufacturer can let the salesperson have a maximum of 20 televisions each week.

   Use an inequality equation to represent the number of televisions that could be sold
   each week if the salesperson meets or exceeds their target. [2]

5. Maisie is thinking of a number (m). $11 < m < 17$
   m is also a prime number.

   What number is Maisie thinking of? [1]

6. Solve the inequality $6x - 2 < 4x + 12$ 🖩 [2]

7. Write down all the integer values of x that satisfy the following inequalities: 🖩

   a) $x > -1$ and $x < 3$ [1]

   b) $x \leqslant 5$ and $x > 2$ [1]

   > **Total Marks** _____ / 12

Quadratic and Simultaneous Equations

1 The area of the triangle is 1.5cm².

Work out the value of x. [4]

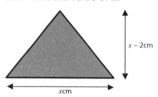

$x - 2$cm

$x$cm

2 The graph below shows the line with equation $y = x^2 - 5x + 6$

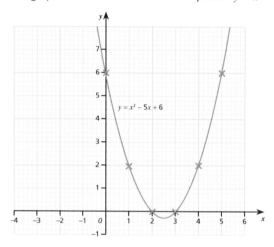

$y = x^2 - 5x + 6$

a) On the same axes, draw the line of the equation $y = 2$. [1]

b) Use the graphs to solve the equation $x^2 - 5x + 6 = 2$ [2]

3 Solve $x^2 + 8x - 9 = 0$ [3]

4 Stephen buys and downloads three apps and four singles at a total cost of £6.10.
Martin buys and downloads five apps and two singles at a total cost of £5.50.

Work out the cost of one app and one single. [4]

5 The sum of two numbers is 20 and the difference is 4.

Set up a pair of simultaneous equations and solve to find the two numbers. [4]

6 The graph has the equation $y = 3x^2$

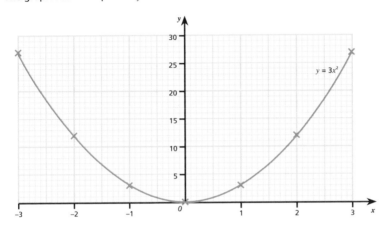

a) On the same axes draw the graph of $y = 4x + 2$ [1]

b) Use your graphs to find estimates to the solutions of the equation $3x^2 = 4x + 2$ [2]

7 Solve the following simultaneous equations:

$2x + y = 1$

$y = x + 2$ [3]

8 Solve the simultaneous equations:

$3x + 2y = 19$

$2x - 2y = 6$ [4]

9 Circle the correct value of a for:

$x^2 + 5x + 6 = 0$

$(x + 3)(x + a) = 0$

$a = 3$ $a = 2$ $a = 6$ $a = 4$ [1]

Total Marks _____ / 29

Answers

Page 5 Quick Test
1. $5(x + 2)$
2. $x = 2$
3. $6y - 5$
4. -171
5. $12t^2 - 3t$

Page 7 Quick Test
1. $w = 9$
2. $(x + 7)(x + 1)$
3. $q = \dfrac{2t + 5}{6}$
4. $y = \dfrac{x + 8}{6}$

Page 9 Quick Test
1. $-4, -8$
2. $-2, 43$
3. 72

Page 11 Quick Test
1. $18, 21$
2. a) $3n + 4$
   b) 154
3. $n^2 - 1$

Page 12
1. $5x + 30$ **[2]** (1 mark for each correct term)
2. $5(3x + 2)$ **[1]**
3. $30 - 12x$ **[2]** (1 mark for each correct term)
4. $4t = p + q$ **[1]**; $t = \dfrac{p + q}{4}$ **[1]**
5. $9x + 4y$ **[2]** (1 mark for each correct term)
6. $4y - 8z + 12$ **[2]**
7. $4x^2 + 2x + 4$ **[1]**
8. 23 **[1]**
9. $8b = 14$ or $2b = \dfrac{7}{2}$ **[1]**; $b = \dfrac{7}{4}$ or $1\dfrac{3}{4}$ **[1]**
10. $3p + 6 = 2p + 6$ **[1]**; $p = 0$ **[1]**
11. $\dfrac{5}{2}x - \dfrac{2}{3}x = \dfrac{1}{2} + \dfrac{1}{3}$ **[1]**; $\dfrac{15}{6}x - \dfrac{4}{6}x = \dfrac{3}{6} + \dfrac{2}{6}$ **[1]**; $x = \dfrac{5}{11}$ **[1]**

> Look for a common denominator.

12. $6x - 30y + 36$ **[2]** (1 mark for 2 correct terms)
13. $6p - 4q + 12$ **[2]**

> $- \times - = +$

14. $4xz(y - 1)$ **[2]** OR $4z(yx - x)$ OR $4x(yz - z)$ **[1]**
15. $(x + 1)(x + 2)$ **[2]** (1 mark for each correct bracket)
16. $6x - 15 + 4x + 12 - 4x$ **[1]**; $6x - 3$ **[1]**; $3(2x - 1)$ **[1]**
17. $A = \dfrac{1}{2}(a + b)h$

Page 13
1. a) i) $20, 23$ **[1]**
      ii) $+3$ **[1]**

b) i) $-4, -8$ **[1]**
   ii) -4 **[1]**
c) i) $\dfrac{7}{9}, \dfrac{7}{27}$ **[1]**
   ii) $\div 3$ **[1]**
2. $24 - 4n$ **[1]**
3. $-2, 1, 4, 7, 10$ **[2]** (1 mark for any three correct)
4. a) $3n + 11$ **[2]** (1 mark for each correct term)
   b) 311 **[1]**
5. a) 23 **[1]**; 30 **[1]**
   b) 3 **[1]**
6. a)

 **[1]**;

b) $2n + 1$ **[2]** (1 mark for each correct term)
c) 201 **[1]**

Page 15 Quick Test
1.

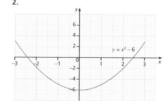

$y = 4x + 1$

2. Gradient $= -2$ and y-intercept $= (0,5)$
3. $y = -1.5x + 14.5$ OR $2y + 3x - 29 = 0$

Page 17 Quick Test
1.

$y = x^2 - 3x + 2$

$(1.5, -0.25)$

2.

$y = x^2 - 6$

3.

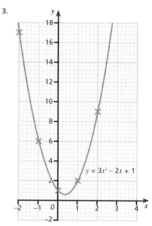

$y = 3x^2 - 2x + 1$

4. Roots $= (-1, 0)$ and $(3, 0)$, turning point $= (1, -3)$

Page 19 Quick Test
1. $y = -2x + 15$
2. 2

Page 21 Quick Test
1.

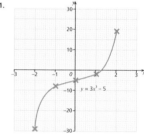

$y = 3x^3 - 5$

2. a) 75 miles
   b) 30 minutes

Page 22
1. $k - g$ **[1]**
2. $12x - 5y$ **[2]** (1 mark for each correct term)
3. $\dfrac{7}{9}$ **[1]**
4. $6 + 10 = 5x - 2x$ **[1]**; $16 = 3x$ **[1]**; $x = \dfrac{16}{3}$ **[1]**
5. $b(5a - 3bc)$ **[1]**
6. $4x - 12 = 10$ **[1]**; $4x = 22$ **[1]**; $x = 5.5$ **[1]**
7. $x = -6$ **[1]**
8. a) $18x + 14$
   b) $18x + 14 = 56$ **[1]**; $x = \dfrac{7}{3} = 2\dfrac{1}{3}$ cm **[1]**
9. a) $r^2 = \dfrac{V}{\pi h}$ **[1]**; $r = \sqrt{\dfrac{V}{\pi h}}$ **[1]**
   b) $r = \sqrt{\dfrac{50}{\pi \times 10}}$ **[1]**; $r = 1.26$ (to 3 significant figures) **[1]**

Page 23
1. LCM of 3 and 4 = 12 **[1]**; therefore, 29 will be common to both **[1]**
2. a)

Pattern Number	Perimeter (cm)
1	5
2	8
3	11
4	14
60	182 **[1]**
n	$3n + 2$ **[1]**

b) $3n + 2 < 1500$ **[1]**; 499 pentagons **[1]**
3. −5, −2, 3 **[2]** (1 mark for one or two correct terms)
4. 66 **[1]**; 130 **[1]**

The difference is doubled each time.

Page 24
1. a)

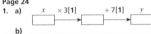

b)

x	−3	−2	−1	0	1	2	3
$y = 3x + 7$	−2	1	4	7	10	13	16

Fully correct **[2]** (1 mark if one incorrect value)
c) Correctly plotted points **[1]**; straight line drawn **[1]**

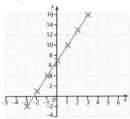

2. a) Sketch showing correct shaped curve **[1]**; correct x-intercepts **[1]**; and correct y-intercept. **[1]**

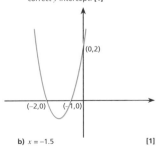

b) $x = -1.5$ **[1]**

3. Fully correct graph with y-intercept at (0, −2) **[1]**; and a straight line crossing through points (−4, −18) and (4,14) **[1]**

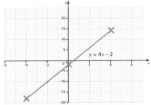

$y = 4x - 2$

4. Fully correct graph with y-intercept at (0, 3) **[1]**; and a straight line crossing through points (−2, −7) and (2,13) **[1]**

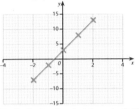

5. Gradient = −2 and y-intercept = (0, 5) **[1]**
6. Fully correct table **[1]**; and accurately plotted graph **[1]**

x	−3	−2	−1	0	1	2	3
y	34	17	6	1	2	9	22

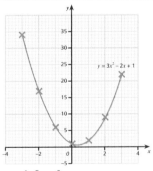

$y = 3x^2 - 2x + 1$

7. $\dfrac{-1 - 5}{3 - (-3)} = \dfrac{-6}{6} = -1$ **[1]**; $5 = -1 \times (-3) + c$, $c = 2$ **[1]**; $y = -x + 2$ **[1]**
8. $m = -1$ **[1]**; $c = 5$ **[1]**; $y = 5 - x$ OR $x + y = 5$ **[1]**

Page 25
1. $m = 3$ **[1]**; $5 = 3 + c$, $c = 2$ **[1]**; $y = 3x + 2$ **[1]**

2. a) Esmai **[1]**
   b) 6mph **[2]** (1 mark for 2 miles in 20 minutes)
   c) 15–20 minutes **[1]**; the part of Gemma's graph with the steepest gradient **[1]**
   d) 12.5 minutes **[1]**
   e) Esmai and Naval are level for first 5 minutes **[1]**; Esmai then speeds up and overtakes Naval **[1]**; Esmai wins, Naval is second and Gemma is third. **[1]** (Accept any other valid points.)
3. $\frac{1}{2} \times 1 \times 30 + 5 \times 30 + \frac{1}{2} \times 3 \times 50$ **[1]**; $+ \frac{1}{2} \times (30 + 50) \times 3$ **[1]**; 360 miles **[1]**

Break the area under the graph down into two triangles, a rectangle and a trapezium.

Page 27 Quick Test
1.

$x < 7$

2. −5, −4, −3, −2
3. a) >
   b) <

Page 29 Quick Test
1. $x =$ (approx.) −1.4 or 3.4
2. $x = 2$, $y = 1$

Page 30
1. $m = \dfrac{5 - 8}{\frac{5}{6} - \frac{2}{3}} = -18$ **[1]**;
   $8 = -18 \times \left(\frac{2}{3}\right) + c$, $c = 20$ **[1]**;
   $y = -18x + 20$ **[1]**
2. $m = \dfrac{4}{2} = 2$ **[1]**;
   y-intercept = (0, 3) **[1]**;
   $y = 2x + 3$ **[1]**
3. $(x + 1)(x + 3)$ **[1]**; $x = -1$ and $x = -3$ **[1]**

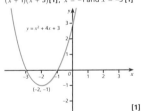

$y = x^2 + 4x + 3$

[1]

4. $m = \dfrac{3}{4}$ **[1]**; $\left(0, \frac{1}{4}\right)$ **[1]**
5. a) $y = (x + 7)(x - 1)$ **[1]**; $x^2 + 6x - 7$ **[1]**; $a = 6$, $b = -7$ **[1]**
   b) −3 **[1]**

Answers

6. a)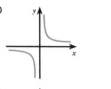

[1]

b)

[1]

7.

[1]

Page 31

1. a) 60mph [1]
   b) Constant speed [1]
   c) $0.5 \times 2.5 \times 60 + 0.5 \times 60 + 0.5 \times 1 \times 60$
   [1]; 75 + 30 + 30 [1]; 135 miles [1]

   Break the area under the graph down into two triangles and a rectangle.

2. a) i) A straight horizontal line [1]
      ii) 30 minutes [1]
   b) 4.30pm [1]
   c) i) $\frac{18}{0.5}$ [1]; 36km/h [1]
      ii) 6pm [1]
3. Gradient = 2 [1]; $y = 2x + c$,
   $6 = (2 \times 3) + c$ [1]; $y = 2x$ [1]

Page 32

1. −1, 0, 1, 2, 3 [1]
2. $2x > 8$ [1]; $x > 4$ [1]
3. $4 \leqslant y \leqslant 12$ [1]; 4, 5, 6, 7, 8, 9, 10, 11, 12 [1]
4. $-4 < x \leqslant 2$ [2] (1 mark for each side of inequality)
5. a) 30 (−6 × −5) [1]
   b) −30 (−6 × 5) [1]
6. a) $x \geqslant 5$ [1]
   b) 2, 1, 0, −1 [1]
7. a) False [1]
   b) False [1]
   c) True [1]

Page 33

1. $x = \pm 3$ [1]

---

2. a) Straight-line graph correct [1]; and curved graph correct [1]

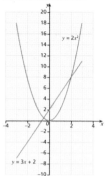

b) $x = -0.5$ [1]; and $x = 2$ [1]

When graphs of simultaneous equations are plotted, the x-coordinates of the points of intersection give you your solutions.

3. $2x + x - 2 = 1$ [1]; $3x = 3$ [1]; $x = 1$ [1]; $y = -1$ [1]
4. a) $(x + 4)(x - 2)$ [1]
   b) $x = -4$ [1]; $x = 2$ [1]
5. $3a + 2p = 220$ and $6a + 2p = 340$ (or equivalent working) [1]; $3a = 120$ [1]; $a = 40$ pence [1]; $p = 50$ pence [1]
6. Add equations to eliminate y [1]; $3x = 12$, $x = 4$ [1]; substitute value for x to find y [1]; $y = 1$ [1]
7. Multiply first equation by 2 and second equation by 3 [1]; $y = 2$ [1]; substitute value for y to find x [1]; $x = 3$ [1]
8. a) Accept values of x from 0.5 to 0.9 [1]; and −2.5 to −2.9 [1]
   b)

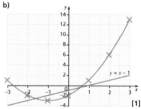

[1]

   c) Accept values of x from 0.4 to 0.8 [1]; and −1.8 to −1.4 [1]
9. $2x = 8$ [1]; $x = 4$ [1]; $8 + y = 9$ OR $16 + y = 17$ [1]; $y = 1$ [1]
10. $x^2 + 3x - 4 = 0$ [1]; $(x - 1)(x + 4) = 0$ [1]; $x = 1$, $x = -4$ [1]
11. $a = 6$ [1]

Page 35

1. $n = 3, 4, 5, 6, 7$ [1]
2. $3x > 21$ [1]; $x > 7$ [1]
3. $3 \leqslant y \leqslant 7$ [1]; 3, 4, 5, 6, 7 [1]
4. If t is number of televisions, $t > 6$ and $t \leqslant 20$ [1]; $6 < t \leqslant 20$ [1]
5. 13 [1]
6. $2x < 14$ [1]; $x < 7$ [1]
7. a) 0, 1, 2 [1]
   b) 3, 4, 5 [1]

Page 36

1. $\frac{1}{2} \times x \times (x - 2) = 1.5$ [1]; $x^2 - 2x = 3$ [1]; $x^2 - 2x - 3 = 0$ [1]; $(x - 3)(x + 1)$, $x = 3$ [1]

   Remember, x is a length in this question so x must be positive.

2. a)

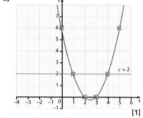

[1]

   b) $x = 1$ [1]; $x = 4$ [1]
3. $(x + 9)(x - 1)$ [1]; $x = -9$ [1]; $x = 1$ [1]
4. $3a + 4d = 610$ and $5a + 2d = 550$ [1]; double equation 2 and subtract [1]; $a = 70$p [1]; $d = £1$ [1]
5. $x + y = 20$ [1]; $x - y = 4$ [1]; $x = 12$ [1]; $y = 8$ [1]
6. a) Correct straight line [1]

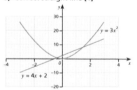

   b) $x = 1.6$ to 1.8 [1]; $x = (-0.5)$ to (−0.3) [1]
7. $2x + x + 2 = 1$ [1]; $x = -\frac{1}{3}$ [1]; $y = \frac{5}{3}$ OR $1\frac{2}{3}$ [1]
8. $5x = 25$ [1]; $x = 5$ [1]; $10 - 2y = 6$ OR $15 + 2y = 19$ [1]; $y = 2$ [1]
9. $a = 2$ [1]

Notes

Graph Paper

Graph Paper